sp◯t

Christmas

The pairs of photos in this book of
picture riddles seem the same...

but look carefully.
There are 7 differences.

You'll also find a **riddle** below each pair of photos.
Need a **clue**? The answer is always something
in the picture above.

Extra Challenge
Looking only at the right-hand pages (and don't forget
the front cover!), find:

1 **rabbit**
5 **candy canes**
13 **sleighs**
18 **snowmen**

and a reindeer's antler (without a reindeer!)

We're best friends.
We're always in and out of hot water,
but it's not like *we're* the ones brewing things up.

Is this a *subpar hint*? Every time I want to say this word, it comes out all mixed up.
Brutish nap! *Turban hips*! It's no use! I have such uncooperative lips!
I can't communicate *a burnt ship. Bah, turnips*!

Hint: An anagram is a word or phrase that can be rearranged to spell something else.
The anagrams in this riddle can all be rearranged to spell the answer to the riddle.

I stand on guard on many legs,
but as for feet, I've none.
And though I'm still, around the field
I run and run and run.

Make no mistake, I've got a tongue,
but I cannot speak or sing.
And though I wear no jewelry,
I'm best known for my ring.

On the starry wind,
Weightless goes the night's hunter,
Lifting silent claws.

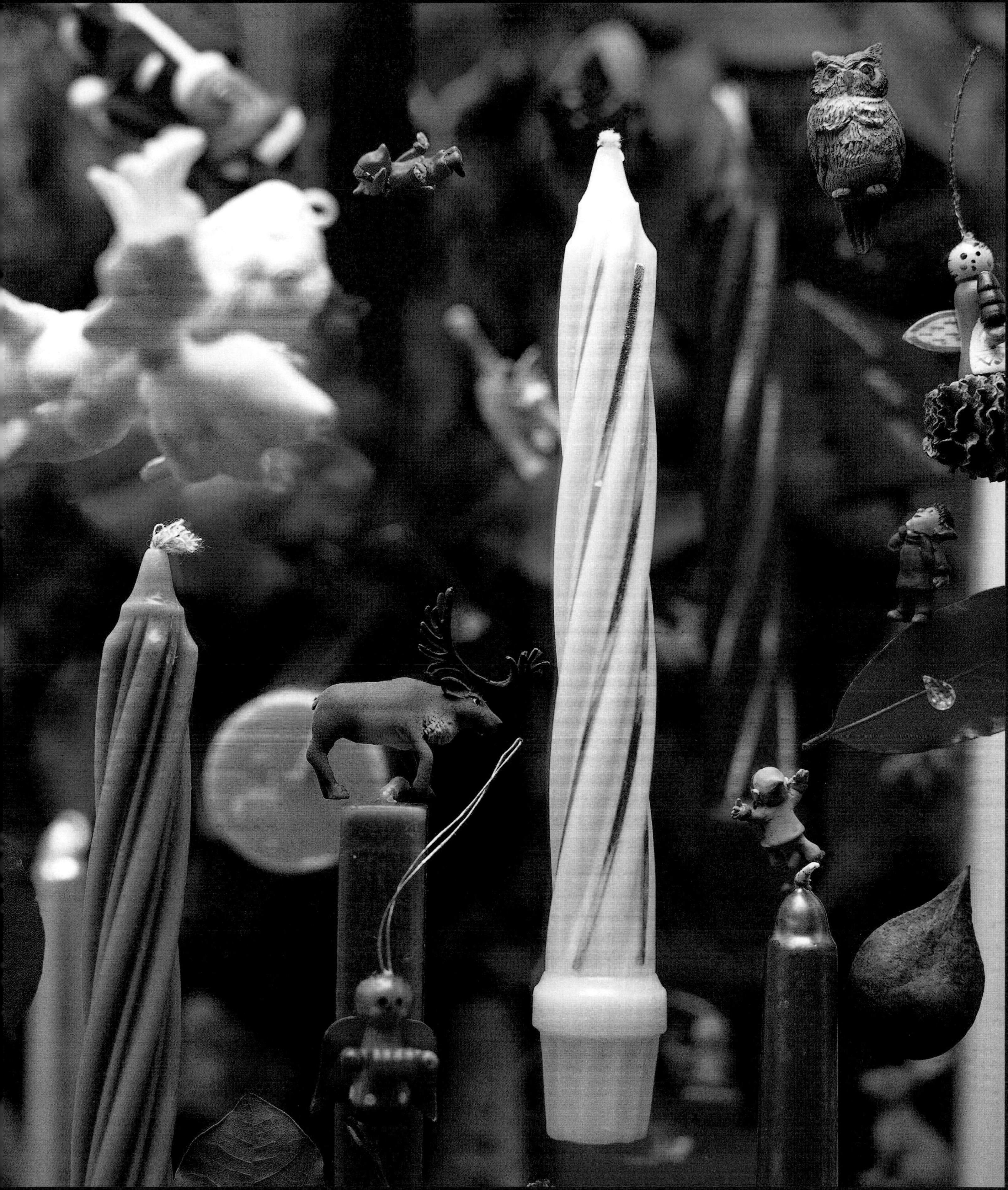

I'm a friend in winter's gray and chilly weather.
But come spring, the strongest tether cannot make me stay.
I'll stream away.

I love feathers best when still attached;
I love to bathe, but dislike wet;
I like to play with my food.
I *hate* the vet.

If you think I look the same as others,
you'd better look again!
Though I have a billion siblings,
not one of them's my twin.

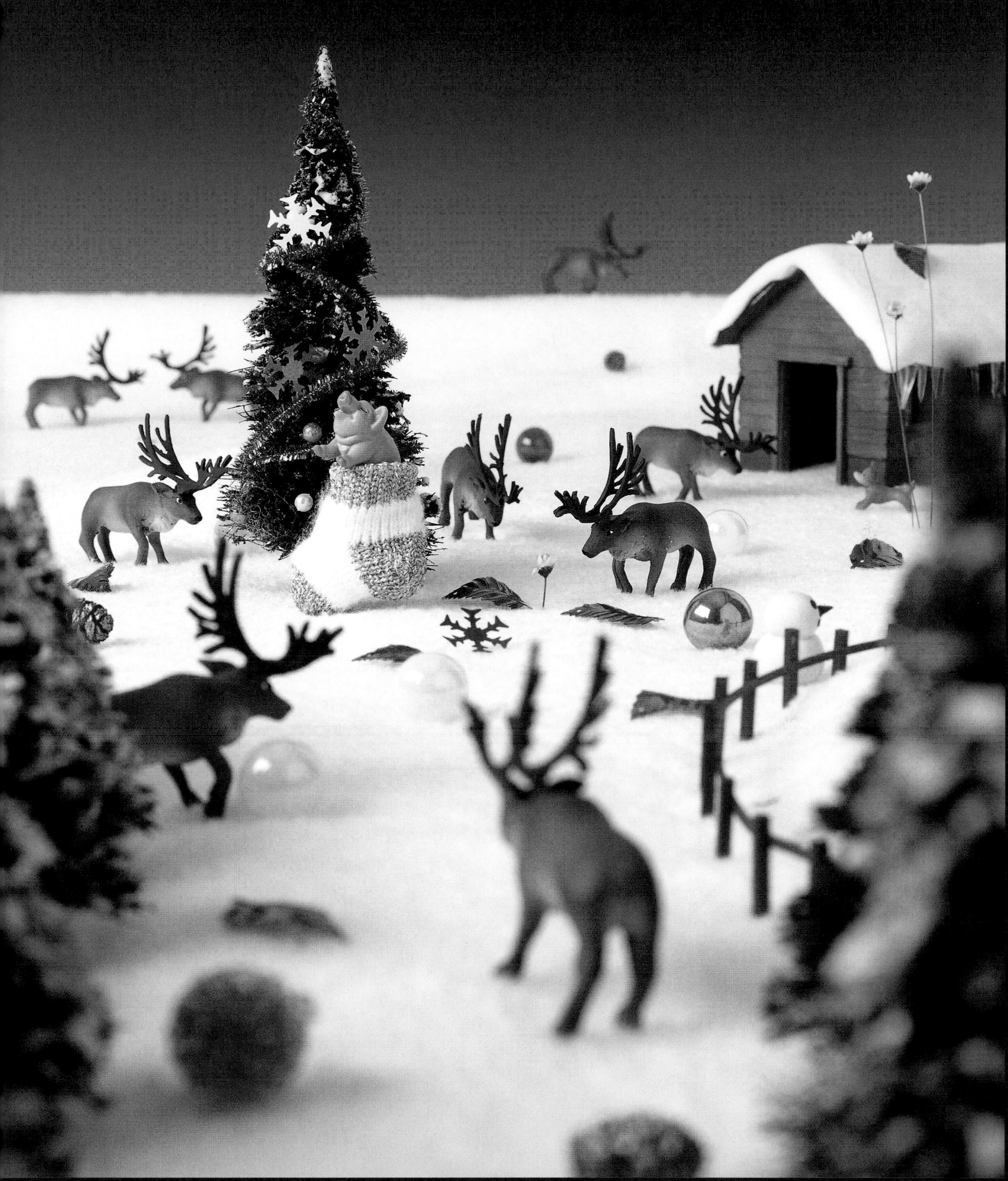

What is it that leans and stands;
has many steps but cannot walk;
is useful, but cannot lend a hand?

I said to the wheel, "Get into gear!"
It spoke, saying, "I can handle myself; don't chain me.
Just have a seat and take a brake."

You can see right through me.
There's nothing I can hide.
But when the wind comes knocking,
I'll not let it inside.

My first is not in honey, but you'll find it in a bee.
My second lives in forests, and is also found in trees.
My last two are in hibernate, but not in den or bite.
My whole will keep you company when you're alone at night.

Hint: This is a spelling riddle.

1._____ 2._____ 3._____ 4._____

Front and Back Covers: Look for

an angel
a pair of glasses
a figure on skates
Santa's teardrop
a star to the right of Santa
something else to the left
a present

Wreaths: Look for

a pair of scissors
one of the chili peppers
a twig with a red berry
a light brown pinecone
a dark brown pinecone
a cup of tea
a little red sleigh bell

Making Cards: Look for

a tube of paint
a snowman
an angel next to Santa
a star on a Christmas tree
a paintbrush
a letter behind Santa
a present on a card

Santa's World: Look for

a Santa in a sleigh
a Santa in an apron
a flower on a path
a bench
an elf lying down
a bottle of soda
something floating in the sky

The Tallest Christmas Tree: Look for

an angel on a horse
a gold pom-pom
a dark green present
a star on the left
a snowflake nearby
a flying reindeer
a Santa on the moon

Candle Lighting Time: Look for

a teardrop on a candle
a twig under an angel
a reindeer
a Santa
something red
a Christmas tree
something brown on the right side

Elves and Bells: Look for

an angel's halo
a snowman's nose
a snowflake on an elf
a snowball on a shovel
a snowman with a scarf
an elf in green
a rabbit

Letters to Santa: Look for

a button by a dog
a Santa on the right
a reindeer's tongue
a Santa in glasses
a Santa on green paper above a moon
a Santa's hat by an elf in red
an extra star on brown paper

Reindeer Outing: Look for

a snowman

a flower

two ornaments in the background

a star

a reindeer on the horizon

a reindeer's nose

Christmas Cakes: Look for

a blue star on a cake

an elf in pink

a cat in a cup

a Christmas tree

an elf in green

something yellow in the background

the place where someone put their
   finger in the frosting (stop that!)

Christmas Eve: Look for

a shooting star

a window that changes color

a present on the right

a white dot by a pink marble

a figure in red on a green ornament

a marionette on a bicycle

a Santa on a sleigh

Down the Chimney: Look for

a silver present

an extra footprint

a figure on a mountain

a Santa with a staff

a present in a sock

a squirrel

a dog on a car

Christmas Morning: Look for

a heart on a card

a heart on a bear

a gold pinecone

an elf in green

a French horn

a present in brown paper

a bow nearby

Answers to the riddles:

Wreaths: cup and saucer

Making Cards: paintbrush

Santa's World: fence

The Tallest Christmas Tree: bell

Candle Lighting Time: owl (this one's an acrostic:
   the first letter of each line spells the answer)

Elves and Bells: snowman

Letters to Santa: cat

Reindeer Outing: snowflake

Christmas Cakes: ladder

Christmas Eve: bicycle

Down the Chimney: window

Christmas Morning: bear

Still can't find them?
Look at our Web page!

http://www.chroniclebooks.com/spot7

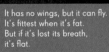

It has no wings, but it can fly.
It's fittest when it's fat.
But if it's lost its breath,
it's flat.

sneak peek!

First published in the United States in 2006 by Chronicle Books LLC.

Copyright © 2003 KIDSLABEL Corp.
English text © 2006 by Chronicle Books LLC.
First published in Japan in 2003 under the title
Doko Doko? Seven 2. Christmas by KIDSLABEL Corp.
English translation rights arranged with KIDSLABEL Corp.
through Japan Foreign-Rights Centre.
All rights reserved.

English type design by Brenden Mendoza.
Typeset in Super Grotesk.
Manufactured in China.

Library of Congress Cataloging-in-Publication Data
KIDSLABEL.
   [Kurisumasu. English]
   Spot 7 Christmas / by KIDSLABEL.
        p. cm.
   ISBN-13: 978-0-8118-5323-1
   ISBN-10: 0-8118-5323-3
1.   Christmas—Juvenile literature. 2. Picture puzzles—Juvenile literature. I. Title.
   GT4985.5.K5313 2006
   394.2663—dc22
   2005028795

Distributed in Canada by Raincoast Books
9050 Shaughnessy Street, Vancouver, British Columbia V6P 6E5

10 9 8 7 6 5 4 3 2 1

Chronicle Books LLC
85 Second Street, San Francisco, California 94105

www.chroniclekids.com

SPot 7